The Plant-and-Grow Project Book

Ulla Dietl

 Sterling Publishing Co., Inc. New York

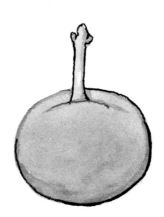
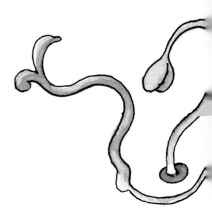

Contents

Library of Congress Cataloging-in-Publication Data Available

2 4 6 8 10 9 7 5 3 1

Published 1993 by Sterling Publishing Company, Inc.
387 Park Avenue South, New York, N.Y. 10016
Originally published in Denmark by Aschehoug Fakta
© 1992 by Forlaget Komma & Clausen Børger A/S
under the title *Spirebogen til små grønne fingre*
English translation © 1993 by Sterling Publishing Company, Inc.
Distributed in Canada by Sterling Publishing
% Canadian Manda Group, P.O. Box 920, Station U
Toronto, Ontario, Canada M8Z 5P9
Distributed in Great Britain and Europe by Cassell PLC
Villiers House, 41/47 Strand, London WC2N 5JE, England
Distributed in Australia by Capricorn Link Ltd.
P.O. Box 665, Lane Cove, NSW 2066
Printed and bound in Hong Kong
All rights reserved

Sterling ISBN 0-8069-0456-9

Preface

I hope this book encourages you to grow plants of all kinds from seeds, cuttings, and sprouts. It does not matter whether you choose house plants or vegetables you'd like to eat. All plants can be beautiful and exciting—in their own way.

The simplest and least expensive method of propagating plants is to force them from the seeds and stones of fruits and vegetables we eat every day. And that's precisely what I show you how to do in this book. With this method, you can "force" rare plants which you cannot easily go out and buy.

For this book, I carried out many simple experiments on my kitchen table. Nothing shown here is really difficult to do. If anything, the activities are quite simple. And most suggestions can be easily followed by children or adults.

Every plant is marked with one, two, or three green fingers to indicate the degree of difficulty. *One finger* is easy—things go quickly. *Two fingers* means the project takes a little more time or can be a little more difficult. *Three fingers* projects require a long time or greater care.

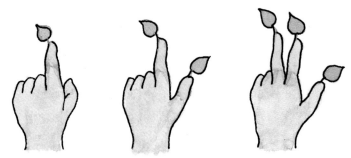

About having a "green thumb" or green fingers, I think this is not something you simply *have*. It's something you acquire, if you care enough about your plants!

—*Ulla Dietl*

Edited by Jeanette Green
Translated from the Danish by Bette Gahres
Illustrated by Ulla Dietl
Photographs by Mogens Steen Jacobsen

Cress

Everyone knows the sprout called cress. Many people have also tried to grow cress themselves and know how easy it is. Scatter the seeds very thickly next to each other on a wet foundation—almost anything works—and the cress grows by itself. Well, if you remember to water it, that is. Without water, no cress.

You can arrange your cress in many different ways, to grow cress pigs, hedgehogs, elephants, and more. The cress creatures look marvelously funny.

However, cress grows best in a shallow tray, such as a TV dinner aluminum tray, a plastic margarine dish, or any shallow dish.

It takes just three to four days to grow your own tray bulging with fresh cress. And this plant will grow year round. The seeds aren't expensive, and you can get many trays of cress from one seed packet.

The easiest way to grow cress is in cotton. Just make sure the cotton is clean, and the cress will grow contentedly. Roll a flat layer of cotton in the tray, and pour water over it until the cotton is completely soaked *before* you scatter seeds on it.

Because cress is cheap and easy to get to germinate, you can amuse yourself by growing it in the strangest materials. Merely having a surface that's a little uneven, the seeds will take root and germinate.

These cress sprouts are greatly enlarged. The big sprout has seed leaves shaped like hands. The little one hasn't straightened itself up yet.

Cress is almost always eaten as sprouts. But the big plant is also very delicious. Cress can get quite tall, develop flowers and large leaves, and still taste good, though the flavor is not as strong.

You can sow your name with cress seeds. Scatter the seeds thinly with ample space between the letters so that the seeds do not grow together. Straighten the seeds with a knife, and remove any seeds that have spilled alongside.

The easiest and cleanest way to propagate cress is to sow the seeds in a thick layer of cotton. You can sow them in all sorts of small containers. Here a disposable drinking glass, a vegetable tray, and a shallow dish have been used.

Eggs and cress taste great together, and they're healthy, too.

Bean Plants

Beans will produce young shoots almost as quickly as cress. Just think of the story of "Jack and the Beanstalk." The scarlet runner bean, shown here, sprouts as soon as it comes near water. Although you can get a scarlet runner bean to sprout in a glass of water, it will die if it's not transplanted to a pot filled with soil.

You can have your own big, beautiful bean plant if you put a bean or two in a flowerpot with soaked soil during the spring. The bean should be almost an inch (2 cm) down in the soil, and the pot should be placed in a well-lit spot. Remember to water it.

The sprout takes 8 to 10 days to come up, and when it reaches 4 to 5 inches (10 to 12 cm) high, it will need a stick or string to grow on.

A scarlet runner plant can grow to several yards (meters) high during the summer. The plant gets red or white flowers and bears bean pods that taste good.

Here several scarlet runner beans have been put in a yellow cucumber, from which they are sprouting. You could also use an apple, potato, or melon.

This is how the bean looks while it's germinating. Just beneath the skin lie the potential leaves and roots.

From one scarlet runner bean you can quickly get a full plant with big, green leaves. In summer, the bean plant can grow around the window several times.

Bean Sprouts Make Healthy Candy

A glass jam jar, a spoonful of bean sprouts, and water two to three times a day is all that you'll need to make a jar full of delicious, crisp bean sprouts. They taste so good that many children would rather eat sprouts than candy. And, besides, they're healthy!

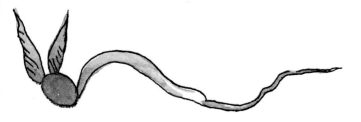

This is how bean sprouts look at about twice their real size. The seeds are very small and do not look alike. That means the squiggly-looking sprouts are not identical either. But they sure taste the same.

Bean sprouts have nothing to do with scarlet runners. Bean sprouts are the funny white sprouts you see in Chinese food and salads. You eat them only as sprouts. They are crisp and delicious. They taste so good that they can be eaten as candy—healthy candy! That's because they contain lots of protein (albumen).

Put a large tablespoon of seeds in a glass jam jar, and lay a thin piece of fabric over the jar's opening. Secure the fabric with a rubber band. Do not use more than one spoonful to a jar, because then the sprouts will not be able to develop. When the sprouts finish growing, in about 4 to 6 days, they will fill the whole jar.

Next, fill the jar with water through the fabric and shake the seeds. Lay the jar in the sink, and *let the water run* out again. Do this two to three times a day until the sprouts are big.

If you want to prepare many bean sprouts at once, say, for a large salad, you use the same procedure. But instead of a jar, use a roasting pan with a dish towel over it.

Bean sprouts will sprout year round, and they sprout best without direct sunlight.

You can prepare a simple salad of bean sprouts with an oil and vinegar dressing. Use just a little vinegar and be generous with the oil. Onion, salt, and pepper are not necessary. The sprouts are tasty in themselves, and the slightly bitter taste makes everything else superfluous.

What Happens under the Soil?

What happens to seeds during germination? Normally you cannot see what's going on, but if you do what we've done here, you can watch the seed develop into a sprout. Usually this all takes place hidden beneath the soil.

Fasten blotting paper with tape to the inside of a clean jar. Fill the jar with sand or soil, not letting any soil get between the paper and the glass. Then add water.

Loosen the blotting paper a little at the top, and place a seed (a bean is good) down between the paper and the glass. If you keep the soil moist, the bean will germinate. And you'll be able to follow the sprout's stages of development through the glass.

9

Grass in the Windowsill

This grass is growing in a wooden tray, lined with thick plastic wrap up to the top. The plastic layer must be watertight, or water will destroy the windowsill.

Perhaps it sounds crazy to have grass in the windowsill, but it looks nice, especially with daisies or other flowers mixed in. And it's fun to watch the grass grow.

If you don't just transplant grass from outside, sow seed in 1¼ to 2 inches (3 to 5 cm) of thick topsoil in a watertight tray. Moisten the soil, and pat it flat with your hands before you scatter the grass seeds over it thickly. Then, pat the seeds down into the soil with your hands. Flower seeds can be put just under the soil.

It's fun to watch the grass sprouts swarm up, and it's exciting if summer flowers appear. The grass can simply stay in the tray until you get tired of looking at it. Just remember to water it. Afterwards, you can plant the grass outdoors, where it will take root. Or you could give it to a little guinea pig or rabbit.

Cat Grass

If you have a cat, you know that it eats grass off and on. Yes, cats can be crazy about grass. After eating grass, the cat usually throws up, but it doesn't look sick. And a little later, the cat eats grass again.

Cats are meat-eaters by nature. When they live in the wild, they live off small animals (mostly rodents) which they eat right after they've been captured. Cats' prey are mostly vegetable-eaters, and that means that cats also eat their supply of green fodder, too. That's if the cat lives outdoors. Domestic cats usually eat meat and fish almost exclusively, with no vegetables. Cats need vitamins and minerals found in greens, and so, they eat grass. That's one reason.

The other reason is that cats are clean animals that lick themselves and their kittens to keep their fur clean and smooth. In the process, they swallow hair, which they cannot digest. Cats throw up this hair when they eat grass (which they cannot tolerate either). In other words, cats eat grass so that they can throw up!

The Cat's Own Plant

If you want to be good to your cat *and* to your plants, you'll make sure your cat always has grass to eat. Otherwise, you run the risk that your feline friend will eat your "real" potted plants. If there isn't any grass near where you live, sow a little *cat grass* in a flower pot.

You can buy cat grass seed at a grocery, pet store, or nursery. You'll get many pots of grass from one seed packet. Put soil in a pot or tray and press it down smooth. Scatter a few seeds thickly (broadcast sowing), and put a little soil or sand over the seeds until they're just covered.

If you water the pot frequently, in about two weeks the grass will be ready to use. Start a new pot as soon as your cat takes over the first one.

Cats sometimes eat potted plants. That may be because they don't have greens in their diet. Give your cat its own flowerpot containing a tuft of grass, and your cat will confine itself to the cat grass.

New Sprouts from Old Vegetables

A little forest of sprouting vegetable tops can be cute and even used as a table decoration. Here cress has been sown around and in the gaps between the veggie tops.

When you buy vegetables in plastic bags, usually the tops have been cut off. But if you remove the top of a carrot, celery stalk, radish, or other root vegetable, you can get the greens to grow again.

Plant the cut-off vegetable top in a shallow dish with soaked cotton or in a flowerpot with soil. Remember to keep the cotton or soil moist all the time, or the vegetable top will die.

The new, fresh green tops will come up in a few days and look sweet. They can be used sprinkled on food or as healthy morsels for your pet.

Onion and Garlic

Onions and garlic also produce fine green tops if you plant them in soil. This can be quickly done with an onion or garlic that's dry.

Plant the onion halfway down the soil, and keep the soil damp. Within a week, a green sprig will come up. You can use it like chives.

You can also grow garlic in a garden or window box simply by sticking dried garlic bulbs a little beneath the soil. Be sure to cover the bulbs with soil. If you do this in the spring, plants will come up during the summer. Homegrown garlic tastes stronger than the store-bought variety.

Celery

Carrots

A small vegetable garden is also good to play with. Here it becomes a "green belt" for a town of wooden houses. The living greens make the little town look more realistic.

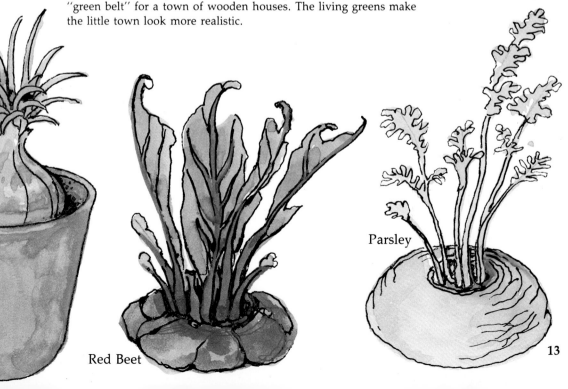

Onion

Red Beet

Parsley

A Cotton Plant

This is how the cotton plant looks with small cotton tufts on it. They almost appear pasted on. Wait until the plant's leaves begin to droop before you pick the cotton. The plant may stay this way for weeks.

Cotton can grow in places that aren't hot. You can easily grow it inside on a sunny windowsill. You probably won't grow enough to weave fabric from it, but you can grow cotton just for fun.

The cotton seed—small and brownish black—can be sown in March or April in a pot with wet soil. Place the seed ½ to 1 inch (1 to 2 cm) in the soil, and it will quickly sprout. The first leaves will be chubby little seed leaves, but soon nicely shaped green leaves appear.

You've probably seen photos of people walking through long rows of cotton plants as tall as they are, collecting cotton in big baskets. Cotton grows well in India and the southern United States. But your window plants will not get that high. However, if the summer is very hot, your cotton plant can readily grow about a yard (meter) high.

The plant quickly produces green buds, which develop into very beautiful yellow flowers and then develop into swelling cotton bolls in the shape of thick, green buds. Around August, every bud "explodes" into a nice creamy white tuft of cotton.

The cotton plant is often an annual. That means it only lives a single summer. So, you should harvest the cotton just when the plant begins to look tired and dreary. Inside every cotton tuft are lots of small, dark seeds, which you can feel but not see. Separate the cotton and pick out the seeds. Or keep the whole cotton tuft, and you'll have plenty of seeds for next year's cotton plant.

In the little pot the first seed leaves have just appeared on the cotton plant. Next to it lie small seeds. The plant behind it is a cotton plant about one month old. A stick supports the plant while it grows.

A cotton plant flowers quickly. These delicate yellow flowers resemble wild roses. The flowers last only a short time and then turn into green bolls.

It's tempting to peek inside the bulging bolls, but don't do it! They open by themselves, and you'll actually hear a little pop when this happens.

When you "harvest" the cotton, save the seeds for next year's cotton plants. The cotton tuft will be full of small black seeds. It's easy to save a whole cotton tuft for next spring.

A Mini-Greenhouse

Mini-greenhouses are inexpensive, and they can be used indefinitely. You can buy peat briquettes in bulk.

You can make a mini-greenhouse or little hothouse with a tray that has a transparent lid over it. In the tray, place thin briquettes made of peat topsoil, and hold them together with a net. In your mini-greenhouse you can force delicate plants or those plants you want to grow quickly. When you plan to use the greenhouse, fill the tray with water. The briquettes will "drink" and expand until they reach the tray rim. Then, one or more seeds can be put in each briquette and the lid placed on the tray. Set the greenhouse in a sunny windowsill.

It's moist and hot in the greenhouse. Moisture condenses inside the lid, falls down, and waters the plants. But you still must water the seeds so they don't dry out.

When the sprouts bump against the lid, take it off. When you transplant each sprout to a pot, transplant the whole briquette, too. Put a pot shard or pebble over the hole in the pot, and be careful with the small roots that stick out.

A greenhouse is partly self-watering.

Plant the sprout in the pot.

A greenhouse provides the ideal climate for germination.

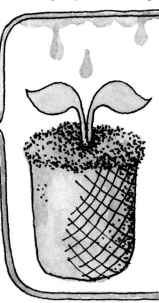

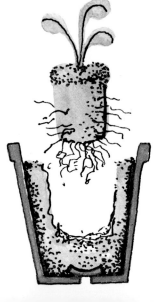

Greenery in the Aquarium

When there aren't any fish in your aquarium, you can use it for plants. In this aquarium, we've covered the bottom with wet cotton and sown it with cress. Nice stones, snail shells, and a little porcelain horse make it resemble a landscape.

Instead of cress, you can place potted cacti in your aquarium. Then cover the bottom with sand all the way up to the pot rims. Add a couple of cowboys and Indians, if you like, and your aquarium will look like the Wild West.

An aquarium also makes a nice greenhouse (hothouse), if you add a glass or plastic sheet for the top. The glass top will make the aquarium self-watering. A closed aquarium also makes a nice terrarium for wild plants.

Bottle Garden

A plant growing in a glass, carafe, or bottle looks decorative, but this won't suit all plants.

All kinds of mosses, ivy, ferns, wild plantains, and runners make the best plants for bottle gardens.

If you want a plant to grow in a bottle or a glass, first put soil or sand in the bottle. Use a stiff paper cone as a funnel to add the soil. This way no dirt will stick to the inside of the glass. Fill about one-third of the glass with soil or sand.

Next, make holes for the plants. You can do this with a long stick, and then drop the plant into place through the cone.

Carefully remove the cone, and use the stick again to carefully press the plant in the ground and cover it with soil. Don't put too many plants into each bottle, and water only when the soil looks dry.

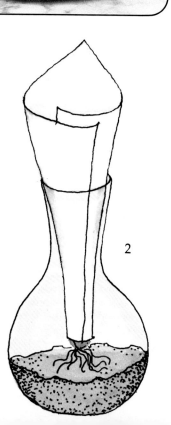

It's not difficult to plant something in a bottle, but you'll need to be careful. It may take an hour to get the bottle to look really nice. Expect plants in bottles to grow a little more slowly than plants in flowerpots.

1

2

3

18

Water Plants

You can make your window view more pleasant with water plants in bottles and glasses. You don't need fish and an aquarium, when you really just want to look at plants.

Find the best-suited bottles and glasses you can. It's best to choose some that aren't too narrow at the top. Preserving jars are especially nice.

First put a layer of sand or peat topsoil in the bottom of the glass and carefully lower the plants. Spread out the roots with a stick if necessary, and lay stones, snail shells, and other things over the roots. Otherwise the roots will come up when you water the plants. If the glass has a narrow opening at the top, you can use a cone to put in the plant to avoid damaging it. Take out the cone before you add water.

Water comes last. Let it slowly run down along the inside of the glass so that you don't stir up the soil and plants.

Water plants should not be fertilized, but be sure they're always covered by water. Carefully fill the container with water when you can see it has dwindled. Growing water plants can be a hobby in itself.

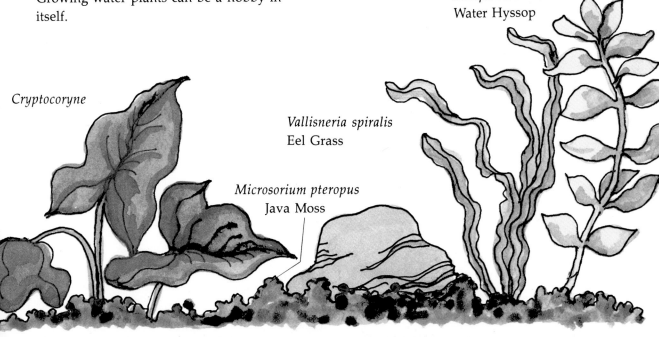

Bacopa caroliniana
Water Hyssop

Cryptocoryne

Vallisneria spiralis
Eel Grass

Microsorium pteropus
Java Moss

You can soak the stone in water for a couple of days or sow it directly with a "sitting plant." The sprout shown has just been transplanted into its own pot.

An Avocado Plant

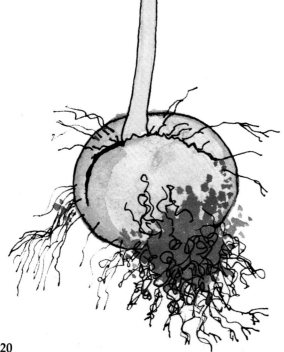

Carefully dig up the sprout with a spoon. Take as much soil and roots with it as possible.

The avocado plant's fruit is black or deep green and pear-shaped. The skin is shiny or dull and bumpy. Inside the fruit is a large, heavy stone (the seed) which can fall out by itself when you cut the fruit in half. If you plant the stone in soil, it will germinate and become a big, beautiful plant.

Since many give advice about how to get an avocado stone to germinate, most people think it's difficult. It isn't difficult if you put the stone in the soil with another plant. You can do this right after you take the stone out of the fruit. If you let the stone "lodge with" the other plant, it's almost guaranteed to germinate. All other methods are doubtful and troublesome.

You need to be patient because the avocado stone takes a long time to germinate. That's why this project gets three fingers. But you'll be rewarded when you see the very vigorous sprout come up.

When the sprout has grown a couple leaves in the "sitting plant's" pot, carefully dig the avocado up, and plant it in its own pot. Keep the soil well watered.

Avoid letting the avocado plant dry out, or its leaves will turn brown. Let it stand in light but not in direct sunlight. If you want the plant to bear fruit, it must do so in a greenhouse.

The avocado plant in the front of the photo is about 9 months old. The leaves have grown large and long. The plant was transferred to a larger pot to grow in.

This three-year-old avocado plant is over a yard (meter) high. Avocado plants can get old and as big as trees, if they are given new soil and larger pots every other year.

When the fruit is ripe, the avocado fruit's flesh is as soft as butter. The taste is mild and quite special. Just eat it right out of the skin and try it with a little salt.

Plants from

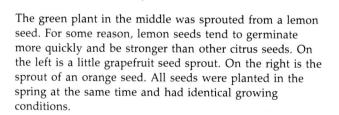

The green plant in the middle was sprouted from a lemon seed. For some reason, lemon seeds tend to germinate more quickly and be stronger than other citrus seeds. On the left is a little grapefruit seed sprout. On the right is the sprout of an orange seed. All seeds were planted in the spring at the same time and had identical growing conditions.

Orange and Lemon Seeds

Fresh seeds from oranges, lemons, mandarins, and grapefruit germinate very readily. You can plant the seeds in soil in early winter and in spring, when citrus fruit (what all these fruits are called) are fresh.

Plant the seeds ½ to 1 inch (1 to 2 cm) in moist soil. Keep the soil moist all the time, without drenching it, or the seeds will rot. Seeds planted around Christmas sprout in early spring. Seeds planted in spring sprout in 14 days to a month.

When the plants are very small, you can already see that they are citrus plants. The "real" leaves come out immediately. Orange and mandarin leaves are long and narrow. The lemon plant has serrated (toothed), chubby leaves.

Citrus plants can get big if they have enough light and heat and if they get enough water and fertilizer. Use fertilizer sticks, not liquid fertilizer.

If the plants become too lanky cut them at the top with scissors. They will then spread out and get bushier.

During summer, the plants may flower. But, unfortunately, it's not the same as having fruit. Citrus plants normally have to be in a greenhouse to develop fruit. But maybe you'll be lucky.

Whether or not you get fruit, ctirus plants are nice to look at.

This lovely mandarin plant wasn't grown at home. It was very small and had tiny green fruit on it when bought. It grew to over a yard (meter) high during the summer. Around Christmas, the fruit seen here was ripe and had a deep orange color. In all, the plant had 35 mandarin fruit on it that tasted sweet and good.

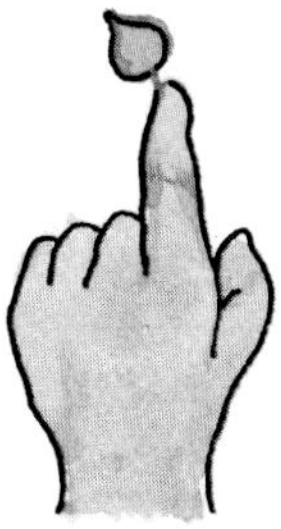

A Potato

Potatoes may be the most ordinary vegetables we have. They're healthy and nutritious and contain lots of vitamin C. Also, they're cheap.

We're so used to potatoes that we don't even think of them as plants. They belong to the nightshade family, to which other plants belong that don't resemble them at all. The tobacco plant, for example, is a member of this family.

Sprouting potatoes appeal to the imagination. Here the sprouts aren't half as long as they can get. They look like strange creatures.

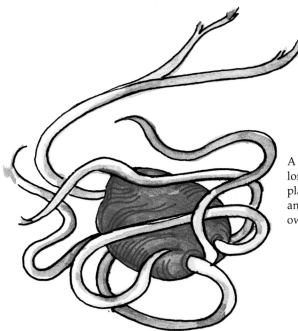

A potato that lies a long time in a dark place gets all shriveled and twisted up in its own sprouts.

Plant

It's a big job, and a lot of soil is needed to grow potatoes for eating. But even if you don't have a garden or window box, you can grow a single potato or two in a flowerpot. A nice, green plant will appear with leaves finer and smaller than it would produce if the potato were grown in a garden.

Remember, though, that only the part of the potato plant that grows *underneath* the ground is edible. If the plant produces berries, do *not* eat them. The berries are poisonous, although not life-threatening.

Sprouting potatoes seem weird creatures, indeed. They can look quite fantastic and resemble trolls, dragons, and monsters of long ago with trunks and antlers.

Potatoes readily produce sprouts when they lie, undisturbed, in a dark place.

An ordinary, store-bought potato laid in a flowerpot with soil grows into a nice green plant with several stems. From time to time, push the soil up around the bare stems.

A Leek Grows

A leek remains vigorous even after it has been dug up out of the ground. Put the leek in a glass of water, and it will continue to grow as though it were still in a vegetable garden. Leeks grow very fast—within a week they can double in size.

It's not only the top that grows, but the roots also get long and winding.

You can't use a leek that has been "played" with in this way for cooking. It will get slimy on the inside and somewhat dry outside. Water in the glass must be changed daily while your experiment lasts. Otherwise, you'll have an onion smell in the room.

Cabbage is another vegetable that continues to grow if you allow it to lie in a cool cellar. It should not be in water. Just let the cabbage lie in peace so that it develops a stalk.

Many other plants can be used for experiments of this kind without wasting good food.

The leek on the right has nearly doubled its size in a week. Watch to see how big a leek can get and how long its roots can grow.

Corn Plants

Corn, like sweet corn or sugar corn, grows best when its sown in pots and forced on a sunny windowsill. Corn plants require a really warm growing place with shelter and sun, both outdoors and indoors.

You can buy the seeds or use raw, home-dried seeds. Plant them ½ to 1 inch (1 to 2 cm) down in moist soil. Plant just one seed to each pot around the middle of April.

In late May the plants can be planted in the garden in the warmest, sunny spot with 24 inches (60 cm) between each plant.

Grow corn plants in the windowsill just because they look nice. You can have a nice, fresh specimen. But, it's unlikely that the cobs the plant produces will bear corn.

With or without *corn on the cobs*, corn plants are worth the trouble to force. This is an inexpensive way to obtain pretty summer plants.

Corn plants should always be started indoors on a windowsill or in a greenhouse (hothouse). But if the plant remains on a windowsill, it's not certain that corn will appear on the cobs.

Here's an outdoor corn plant with a tassel at the top. Cobs develop in the axils in about 75 days.

Young corn plants have fine, slender leaves. A little corn forest in the windowsill can be decorative.

European chestnut trees have distinctive leaves which you can peel and make "herringbones" from.

Chestnut Tree

Every fall, children and adults in Europe and North America collect bright, shiny chestnuts along streets and in forests. You'll have to be quick to get some!

Just don't make necklaces and animals from all your chestnuts. Set aside a few for sprouting. It's easy enough to get a chestnut to sprout, but the budding plant takes its time. That's why this project gets three green fingers.

Put soil in a tray. Garden soil is fine since chestnuts aren't delicate. Moisten the soil and half bury the chestnut in it.

Water the soil throughout the winter only when the soil is dry. Allow the tray to sit undisturbed, preferably in a cool spot. Move the tray into the sun just before spring.

The big, vigorous chestnut sprout breaks through the shell in spring and grows well. During the summer you'll have a nice big "tree."

A shortcut in growing a little tree is to find a chestnut that has sprouted in the forest in late spring.

Carefully lift the sprouting chestnut out of the ground so that you can see the root shoots. After the chestnut sprouts, gently transplant the tiny tree to a big flowerpot with good potting topsoil.

Toothpick "Horse" Chestnut

Sprouting Hazelnut

In October, hazelnut bushes drop their nuts, and that's when some European families go nut hunting. If you find a good place, you can gather all you'll need in an afternoon.

You can plant a couple nuts that you collect in a pot with soil. Do not crack them—plant them whole. Hazelnuts don't require heat during germination. If anything, they need the opposite. Don't place the pot in a heated windowsill. Let it stay in a cool spot undisturbed through winter. Water this seed only when the soil looks dry (test it with a finger).

When spring arrives, move the pot to a light and warm windowsill. Hazelnut bushes do *not* grow quickly in pots, and you won't harvest any nuts from them. Only if you plant the bush in a garden or in the wild will it yield nuts. As a potted plant, a hazelnut bush resembles a young birch. If you trim and prune the plant now and then, it will be fuller.

Sprouting hazelnut kernels like this one can be found every spring around outdor hazelnut bushes. If you put the hazelnut in a pot with fertilized topsoil and cut it often at top, it can turn into a nice indoor miniature bush.

This date palm is barely three years old. In the middle, a new leaf is coming up.

Date Palm

If you save a date stone from a snack, you can force a date palm tree. Put the nut in soil right after you eat the date. Plant it with another plant you have watered beforehand. It's not difficult to force a date palm, but it does take a long time. That's why it gets three green fingers.

The stone takes a couple months to sprout into a thick blade of grass which quickly divides into two. The first year the plant grows very slowly. Fertilize the date palm when it is a year old.

The date palm survives under conditions that would cause other plants to die. It tolerates partial shade and can be frugal with water. Gradually, the palm develops more leaves and can get very old. If you move your date palm to a bigger pot about every other year, the little tree will get very big.

This is how the palm looks at five years old. It will be about a yard (meter) high at that age.

Mimosa

In peace and quiet, the delicate mimosa's leaves unfold.

A child's hand touches the mimosa, and its leaves immediately fold up. You can watch them slowly close.

Mimosa is a delicate plant. The little shrub is so delicate that when you touch the leaves, they fold up. A wind gust or a light shake can also be enough to disturb this sensitive plant.

When left alone, the mimosa's fine lobed leaves are beautifully unfolded, but if you touch or water it, the leaves fold up. What actually happens is that the sap level in the mimosa's leaves and branches drops, so they become limp. They again fill up with sap after the disturbance is over. Why the plant reacts the way it does, we don't know.

The mimosa is also sensitive to light. When it gets dark, the plant closes up.

The mimosa gets three fingers, because keeping this plant alive in cool northern latitudes is difficult. In its native country, Brazil, the mimosa gets sufficient heat and moisture and grows to the size of a bush. Elsewhere mimosa is an annual, and may, if you're lucky, last a summer.

After you sow the mimosa seed, it germinates quickly if it has enough light and water. This is an interesting plant that fascinates both children and adults.

These wheat sprouts are almost too old to eat. If they're not eaten soon, they'll end up as window decoration.

Wheat Sprouts

Whole wheat grains, which you can buy in health food stores or find in coarse flour, sprout readily.

Broadcast sow wheat grains by scattering them thickly in a tray with soil. Pat the soil smooth a little before you scatter the seeds. Then scatter a thin layer of soil over them after sowing. Water them at the same time. Continue to water the wheat sprouts diligently while they grow.

If the tray stands in light, germination occurs quickly. In 2 to 3 weeks the wheat grain sprouts become the right size. The sprouts resemble thick blades of grass. Cut and use the greens in salads, and sprinkle them on rice dishes.

These delicious and healthy greens are rich in vitamins. Eat them while they're tender. Wheat sprouts can become tough and lose their tasty crispness quickly.

If you allow the sprouts to stand too long, you'll get a "wheat field." And that may be nice to look at, but you cannot eat it.

The pitcher is full of peppermint and lovage with yellow flowers. The small pot contains lemon balm, brought in from the garden. All herbs thrive outside. The larger pot contains basil. Herbs are also lovely to have as ornamental plants.

Potherbs

Most potherbs can be sown. Some, however, do better if you buy them as tubers or small plants. Potherbs thrive in sheltered sun, where they develop into big, usable plants. The Mediterranean herbs thyme, marjoram, basil, and rosemary especially need sun, while familiar herbs like chervil, parsley, and lovage manage under harsher conditions.

You can sow herb seeds in a mini-greenhouse (hothouse) or in small pots with a sheet of glass over them. When the herbs are 4 to 5 inches (10 to 12 cm) high, you can move them out into the garden or to a flower box in sheltered sun. These potherbs can also stay in the windowsill.

But if you grow them there, be sure to repot them to bigger pots with more soil so that they can develop properly.

When you want to use greens from potherbs to season food, simply cut off the top shoots (scissors work best). That way, the plant can branch out and get bushy, even if you cut from it constantly.

Both the leaves and stalk of some herbs can be used. For others, only the leaves are used. But you'll soon learn that, if you taste them yourself.

Some herbs are perennials; others live only a single summer. Consult the seed packs.

A Banana Tree

The banana tree probably originated in Malaya, Southeast Asia. Banana belongs to the *Musa* family, and the plant is not a palm, as many suppose, but a gigantic herb. Bananas once came from Spain and West Africa. Today most bananas we eat come from Latin America—Panama, Honduras, Costa Rica, Colombia, and Ecuador.

In its native countries, the banana tree grows colossally large—three to five times as high as a man—and has 30 to 50 bananas on each bunch. Banana plants need lots of heat and water. That's why they grow best in tropical climates with rich topsoil and swampy or marshy soil.

We can get banana plants to grow in temperate (cooler) climates, and banana seeds can germinate in a sunny windowsill under a sun catcher or in a greenhouse. But we cannot force bananas. To force bananas, you need a tropical (hot) climate or a large hothouse. It doesn't matter how big the plant gets. The fruit simply will not grow.

The banana tree's seeds are big and black. Plant them in a flowerpot or tray with soil that's always moist. Find a sunny spot, and it's best to place a glass or plastic lid over the pot's opening. A mini-greenhouse (see p. 16) is well suited to forcing banana plant sprouts. When the sprout comes up, it resembles a thick, wavy blade of grass. This "blade" quickly divides into several pointed leaves and grows well.

Even in a cool climate, the banana plant can develop into a giant plant. This little tree grew from about 12 inches (30 cm) to become about a yard (meter) high in one year. The boy standing next to the plant is 4 feet (120 cm) tall.

The banana tree's seed looks peculiar. It's about ½ inch (12 mm) wide and resembles a baboon's nose. Since getting the seed to sprout can be difficult, you may prefer to buy a little tree.

If you want to play it safe, you could buy a little banana tree to begin with.

Even in cool climates, the banana tree becomes a very big potted plant if you repot it in successively larger pots as it grows. Fertilize the little tree well. If you have access to horse manure, your banana tree will do well.

It's not easy to say how old a banana tree can get in a windowsill. If the tree is not exposed to frost (it dies immediately from frost) and stays warm, it can become two to three years old. But do not expect to have your banana tree much longer than that. In return, while the banana tree lives, it can develop into the biggest potted plant you can think of. Before the tree dies, it will produce one or more root suckers close to the stem. These offshoots can become new banana trees!

Almost as though the banana tree knows it will soon die, it produces a little root sucker to reproduce itself. When the mother tree dies, the root sucker is ready to take over the flowerpot.

Eucalyptus Tree

Eucalyptus is an exciting tree, but it's also a little difficult. That's because it only grows in full light. You'll need to sow the seed or buy a finished plant. You cannot propagate the plant from cuttings. Use a mini-greenhouse for forcing it from seeds.

As a big potted plant, the eucalyptus tree drinks a lot of water. It grows quickly and can become several yards (meters) high. Although the tree tolerates direct sun and low temperatures in winter, it can die from frost.

The branches do not divide. When you touch the blue-green leaves, they release a strong, fragrant eucalyptus oil. This magnificent little tree requires care, however. It should never dry out or stand in shade. Many species of eucalyptus thrive in Australia.

The eucalyptus tree shown in the photo is about a year old. It was forced from seed.

After about two years the tree begins to grow steadily and must be watered often. The leaves are opposite and without a stem. On a big tree the leaves can easily be 4½ to 6 inches (12 to 15 cm) long. Support the eucalyptus tree with a strong stake.

Eggplant

The eggplant (aubergine) can be sown indoors in small pots in February. When the sprouts are big enough, repot each in its own pot. Choose a warm and sunny place, and give the plant a big pot, good soil, and lots of water.

Support the plants with a stick when they are half grown, or they could break when they bear fruit. The fruit will be ready to harvest in the summer, and if you plan to eat them, harvest the fruit when it turns deep purple.

If you want to be sure to get fruit, some gardeners advise nipping off the plant's first flowers.

Here we've allowed the fruit to hang on the plant because it looks nice.

The dark dots in the split eggplant are seeds. They can be eaten, too. You can rub the fruit with salt before you use it in casseroles or fry it with onions and tomatoes.

Eggplants are related to tomatoes. The eggplant flowers resemble the tomato plant's flowers.

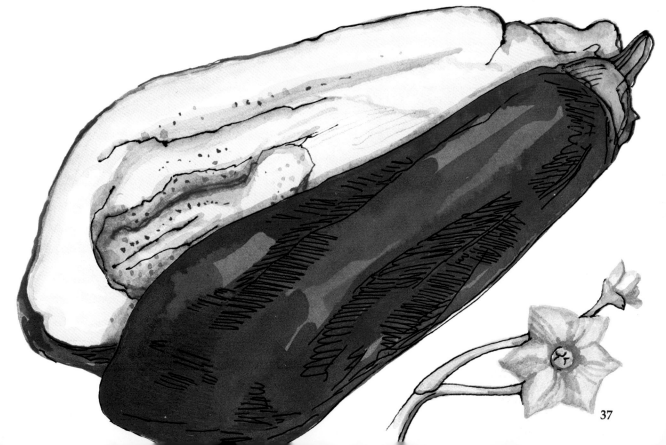

This split open green pepper is full of seeds. Every seed can become an independent plant, which will bear fruit. Green peppers are actually unripe but edible. Ripe peppers are red or yellow red. You can eat peppers as soon as they break when you squeeze them.

Plants from

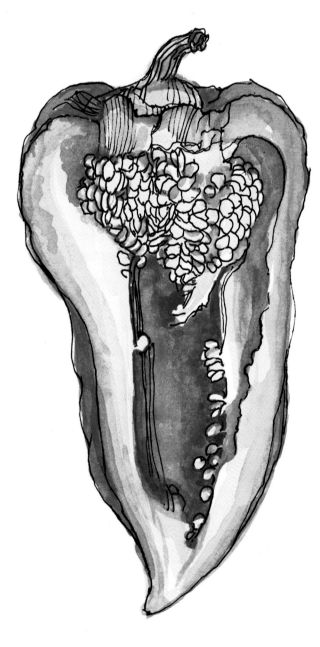

The pepper plant is a cousin of the tomato. We use peppers in casseroles, salads, and other dishes. When you're ready to use the fruit, remove the white seeds inside.

Instead of throwing these seeds out, plant them in a tray with moist soil. Within a week you'll get a whole tray full of little, vigorous sprouts. Every sprout can become a plant with peppers of its own. Pepper plants don't need to be in a greenhouse to produce fruit. They thrive well in a windowsill, as long as they get a little sun.

When the sprouts get high enough to hamper each other in the tray, transplant them. Give each sprout its own pot. Use only the best sprouts.

Since pepper plants drink a lot of water, even when small, water them as soon as they look a little dry. When the plants are 4½ to 6 inches (12 to 15 cm) high, you can fertilize them and give them a stick for support.

Several peppers can grow on each plant during the summer, but they won't become as big as the peppers you buy. Pepper plants should not be pruned.

Pepper Seeds

Pepper seeds can be planted in moist soil immediately. Plant seeds with a little space between each and cover them with a thin layer of soil. The plant next to the boy is about 1½ months old. The fruit is almost ready.

When the pepper sprouts get to about this size, they're ready for transplanting, each sprout to its own pot. The sprouts here were sown in a cress tray.

The children in this class have grown date, avocado, eggplant, tomato, pepper, squash, and corn plants. They've also grown many herbs, like chives, parsley, and cress.

Classroom

Why not grow plants in your classroom? It's really quite easy and fun. Plant projects and experiments can be carried out everywhere. Teachers and students enjoy the built-in learning possibilities these projects have and how easy it is to integrate them with other subjects, like science or art.

This third-grade class in Denmark has grown various vegetables and herbs through the spring and summer. Children took turns taking care of the plants and windowsills. They could either take care of their own individual plant or check a calendar kept on a bulletin board that showed whose turn it was each week. Two or three children or the teacher and one child tended the plants. During vacations, children took the plants home with them.

Some plants were grown from bought seeds, others from the seeds of fruits and vegetables used in cooking class. The children have even succeeded in forcing generous plants that have borne fruit.

Growing plants became part of other school subjects—even home economics. In art class, the children made saucers and nice pot covers for their plants.

In addition, the plant projects have encouraged the children to talk and work together.

These students studied growing plants, and this study was integrated with other subjects. Each child had his or her own files to illustrate and tell about plant families, seed development, and various stages and uses of plants.

Offshoots and Cuttings

This hard-working plant is eager to produce roots as cuttings and to flower. It has formed more roots than necessary to be transplanted to their own pots.

It's fun to see if you can take an offshoot from a plant. There are many ways to do it, and there is a method that works best for each plant. You can propagate some plants only from seeds, and from others you can take cuttings or offshoots. The methods described below are the most successful.

The **cuttings** method is simple. Take a healthy and vigorous shoot from the plant and put it in water. Cut off the shoot with a sharp knife. If the cutting forms roots within 8 to 14 days, the propagation has succeeded. Then the little plant can be moved to its own pot.

Leaf cutting is also an easy way. Take a leaf or a top shoot from a plant, and plant it directly in wet soil. The shoot forms roots by itself and grows to be a plant. This method is good, for example, for cacti, succulents, and similar plants.

Leaf division is a little more complicated. Cut a leaf, like mother-in-law's tongue, into pieces with a sharp knife. When the flat cuts are dry, put the pieces into moist soil, where they form roots.

Stem propagation can be achieved by some plants by themselves. Runners (*Chlorophyta*), spider plants, piggyback plant, and some orchids push out stems, with small plants on them, that are ready to be put into pots of their own.

Root division works with ferns and some other plants. Take the plant out of the pot, and carefully divide it into two or more plants. It's a little more difficult than other methods because the root system is delicate.

Some gardeners think cuttings should be stolen to thrive well. Of course, that's nonsense. Some plants cannot be propagated by cuttings, and may even be damaged or killed this way. Always find out whether this method is suitable for the plant in question.

Stem propagation happens automatically. You can transfer small plants to their own pots immediately. Also, you can let the cuttings take root in a pot while they are still part of the parent plant.

Leaf division can work with mother-in-law's tongue (*Sansevieria trifasciata*). Offshoots or clones won't have yellow markings.

43

Offshoots and Cuttings

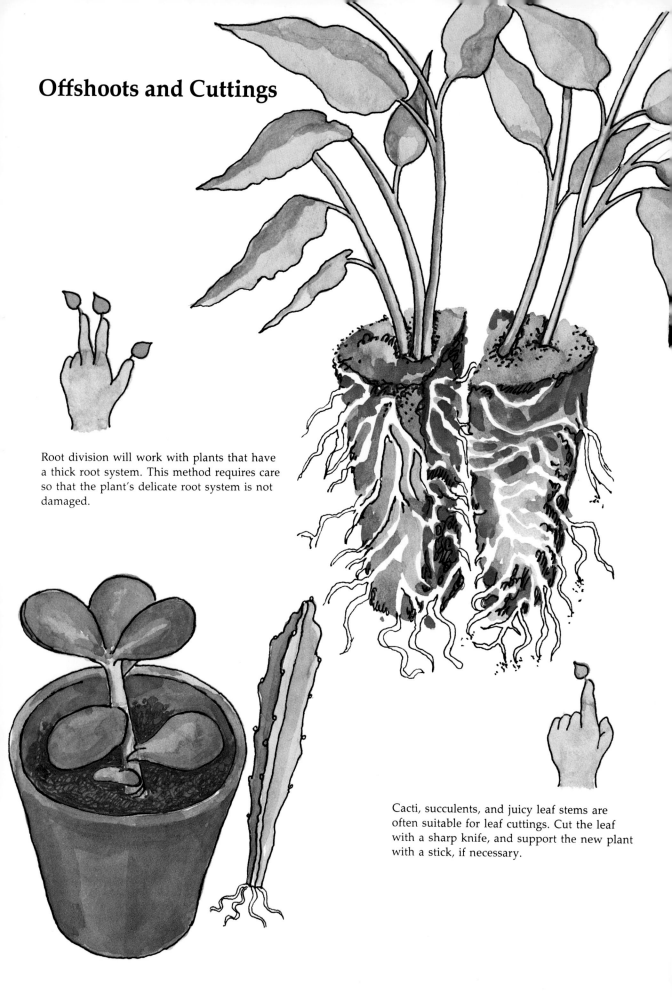

Root division will work with plants that have a thick root system. This method requires care so that the plant's delicate root system is not damaged.

Cacti, succulents, and juicy leaf stems are often suitable for leaf cuttings. Cut the leaf with a sharp knife, and support the new plant with a stick, if necessary.

Tips about Plants

When is the best time to germinate?

Some seeds, like cress and bean sprouts, germinate all year round. But most seeds germinate only in the spring or early summer. Seeds, like date stones and avocado stones, can also hibernate. Most seeds germinate in darkness (soil), but cress, grass seed, and beans also germinate in the light.

Light

All plants seek light when they come up. They manage best on a windowsill or in another place where light is available. A few plants can tolerate shade, but all plants in this book prefer light.

Sun

Very few plants tolerate standing in baking sun. These include cacti, cotton, and corn. Most plants thrive best in light with a little sunlight now and then. If a plant gets too much sun, it "faints."

Tips about Plants

Air

Plants breathe through leaves and roots. That's why it's important to pour away any excess water that remains in the saucer when you water the plant, about ten minutes after watering. And no plant can tolerate standing in a constant draft.

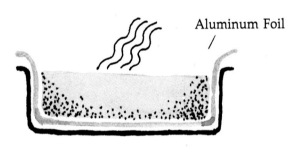

Aluminum Foil

Sick Plant

You can give new soil and new pots to plants which have drooping leaves, dry leaves, or seem to be losing their leaves. This can help. Check first to make sure the cause isn't just a lack of water or that the plant has gotten too much water. Lice and vermin can be removed by sprinkling the plant with lukewarm water. Don't forget the backs of leaves. As a rule, this must be done several times before the bugs or other pests are gone.

Water

All plants should be watered, including cacti. A plant that sits in the light where it's dry needs more water than one that sits in the dark. Plants should be watered when the soil feels dry. Test the soil with a finger, and get into the habit of keeping an eye on your plants. Too much water "drowns" the plant. See Air.

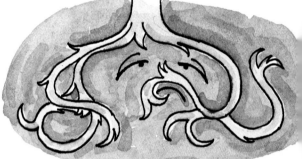

Soil

The plant soil that you buy at supermarkets and florists is the easiest to use. Garden soil that isn't too stony or clayey can also be used, but sterilize it first: Put the soil in a roasting pan lined with aluminum foil (not paper or plastic). Set the oven at about 250 degrees F (120 degrees C) and bake the soil for an hour. Let the soil cool before sowing or planting in it.

Fertilizing

Plants grow faster and get bigger when they are fertilized. Liquid fertilizer is difficult to use. Try fertilizer sticks. Simply put the stick in the soil so the plant can take what fertilizer it needs by itself. Follow the directions on your packet.

Sprouts should *never* be fertilized. Wait until the plant has produced several leaves.

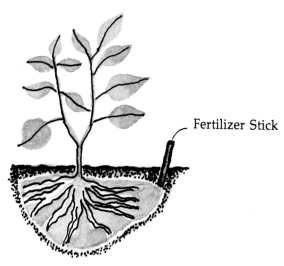

Fertilizer Stick

Pots

Clay pots are good, but they're also expensive. Plastic pots, foil trays, and vegetable trays are also fine. Even tin cans can be used, but avoid those with sharp edges. Make a hole in the can with a nail so that the water can run out. Use plastic lids or something similar as saucers.

Resuscitation

If a plant is completely dried out, you can try to save it by placing it in water "up to its neck" for an hour. Afterwards, cut away the withered leaves and stems, perhaps even all the way down to the stump. Some plants will then grow new leaves and stems and start all over again. Those you cannot save should be thrown out, but wait a few weeks first to see what happens.

Index